Original title:
You Can't Find the Meaning of Life on Amazon

Copyright © 2025 Creative Arts Management OÜ
All rights reserved.

Author: Arabella Whitmore
ISBN HARDBACK: 978-1-80566-154-2
ISBN PAPERBACK: 978-1-80566-449-9

Quantum Queries in an Online World

In the depths of search bars wide,
I seek wisdom, my loyal guide.
Yet every click a riddle spun,
From cat memes to the latest gun.

I scrolled for answers, oh what a quest,
But found only socks and a treasure chest.
Algorithms dance, a wild parade,
Philosophy lost in a coupon trade.

With each bright button I must resist,
I ponder truth, I can't persist.
Wrapped in boxes, joy's fleeting jest,
My inner sage says, "Just take a rest!"

A cosmic joke in a digital realm,
Where wisdom's drowned, with tweets at the helm.
Yet laughter greets me, as I scroll along,
For what's life's meaning? It's in the throng!

Return Policies of Reflection

In a cart, I placed my dreams,
With warranties, or so it seems.
But when I sought that perfect grace,
I found it lost in cyberspace.

Return them all, my hopes in tow,
Refund my time, let wisdom grow.
These policies, they keep me sane,
But what of joy? Can it be gained?

Escaping the E-Commerce Labyrinth

I searched for meaning, clicked and scroll,
Trapped in a maze of soulless mall.
A door, a wall, just more cellophane,
Where's the exit from this mundane?

The basket fills with things I need,
Yet none can plant a hopeful seed.
With every deal, my heart does sink,
What's in the cart? Just thoughts to think.

Unsearched Spaces of the Heart

Forgotten realms lie in my chest,
Not on the site where promos rest.
browse my feelings, what a chore,
I'd rather shop for socks galore.

Yet hidden gems are waiting there,
In pillow talks and laughter shared.
No shipping fees for love's embrace,
Why can't I find that special place?

Aisles of Ambiguity

Among the shelves of 'what if' dreams,
I wander lost in silent screams.
Should I select or leave it be?
These aisles mock my clarity.

I add to cart, then hit rewind,
Last minute thoughts, they're unrefined.
Life's not a product, that much I know,
But shopping's just easier, go with the flow.

Beyond the Cart and into the Cosmos

Clicking through joys, I roam the site,
But answers to questions just aren't in sight.
A search for wisdom, I thought I could snag,
But found only socks, and a weird-looking flag.

Scrolling and scrolling, my time slips away,
Lost in a maze where I thought I could play.
'Add to the cart,' it calls like a song,
Yet meaning eludes me, all night long!

Wandering Offline

Battery dying, I step out the door,
Looking for meaning, I trip on the floor.
The sun sees my struggle, my waning delight,
While Wi-Fi signals dance just out of sight.

I chat with a squirrel, he nods with a grin,
Maybe he knows where the answers begin.
But he only offers a nut and a friend,
And I leave understanding nothing to send.

Navigating the Void of Consumerism

Adding to my cart like it's a black hole,
Hoping it fills up that empty old soul.
With gadgets and gizmos, I bask in the gleam,
But lights don't bring clarity; they dim my dream.

At checkout, I ponder, with items galore,
Can a salad spinner help me explore?
A map of life, or perhaps just despair,
Yet here I am, with a spatula to share.

Beyond the Clickbait

Endless distractions from day into night,
Chasing illusions, I lose the true light.
A headline screams, 'Live your best life now!'
But it's full of clickbait, I'll take a bow.

In search of deep meaning, I browse and I scroll,
Yet find only memes that take toll on the soul.
So I drop my device, let my brain take a jog,
Who knew that was easier than buying a blog?

Discounts on Truth

Searching for wisdom on a big site,
Only to find gadgets that spark delight.
I added some joy to my virtual cart,
But deep down I knew, that's not true art.

Free shipping on doubt, but what's the cost?
My clarity dwindled, it seemed so lost.
Refunded my worries, but they reappear,
Turns out they're not prime, just lingering here.

Wishlist of the Soul

Made a wish list for what fills my heart,
A toaster, a lawn chair, and a bit of smart.
Yet when I clicked purchase, what came to view?
A rubber duck and a shirt that's too blue!

Items in my cart, fun socks and a book,
But where's that deep stuff? Let's take a look.
It turns out the meaning just slips from my grasp,
Like bubbles in soda, they fizz and they gasp.

Prime Deliveries and Forgotten Whispers

Clicking 'buy now' for a laugh and a cheer,
But wisdom don't ship in two days, I fear.
Tracking my thoughts like a delivery guy,
But still, the big answers seem to drift by.

I've got bubble wrap thoughts and a box of old dreams,
Unpacking my heart with a side of ice creams.
Yet still, I find silence in each cardboard pile,
Perhaps there's a treasure, wrapped up in a smile.

Unpacking the Weight of Being

Unboxing my life like it's just a new gadget,
Finding old gifts wrapped in a memory bandage.
The manuals are missing, but hey, that's alright,
I'll wing it with laughter and dance through the night.

Heavy with joy, yet I'm light as a feather,
Digging for purpose in all kinds of weather.
With each quirky find, I'll discover, I bet,
The fun is the journey, not how to forget.

Existence is Not Prime

In a world built on clicks,
Where wisdom's just a sale,
Searching for truths in boxes,
More likely to fail.

A toaster with 12 settings,
Saves me from my fate,
Yet pondering my being,
Is not on the slate.

Instructions lost in shipping,
No tracking for the soul,
Algorithms can't help us,
To feel truly whole.

So laugh at the absurdity,
Life's not a quick buy,
For answers you won't find here,
Just checkout and goodbye!

Beyond Checkout: A Journey

Step right up for wisdom,
But first, add to your cart,
A sprinkle of deep meaning,
Just charged to your heart.

Click the box for laughter,
Or choose the path of tears,
Life isn't in the widgets,
It's tangled in your fears.

Need a guide for this journey?
Try primes, two-day delivers,
But cosmic enlightenment,
Won't come from free shivers.

So brace against the nonsense,
In each aisle, take a peek,
Real gold can't be shipped, my friend,
It's found when you're unique!

The Cart of Cosmic Questions

An empty cart is waiting,
For ponderings of the mind,
Can I check out some answers,
Or is life just unkind?

Add deep thoughts for free,
But they won't fit in a box,
Shipping's slow on wisdom,
With plenty of roadblocks.

Searching for the meaning,
Via online retail spree,
Each click leads to wonders,
Still lost on A, B, C.

Life's not an order form,
With a price tag on the side,
Embrace the quirks and questions,
And let the laughter glide!

Discontinued Dreamscapes

Once ordered dreams by night,
Now they've all been recalled,
They said, 'Out of stock on meaning,'
Though my hopes were enthralled.

Return policies are tricky,
When the heart starts to ache,
Life's not just a wishlist,
But more like a mistake.

In the warehouse of existence,
They've closed down all the doors,
The only thing in inventory,
Is laughter, maybe scores.

So let's check out the nonsense,
Two-for-one on a grin,
In a world of wild surprises,
The fun must now begin!

Order Confirmation for the Unknown

Add to cart, a quest for truth,
With discounts on wisdom, who needs proof?
One-click to find the reason to be,
But checkout's a mystery, we wait to see.

In a warehouse of thoughts all packed tight,
Shipping our dreams, on a whim, day and night.
Returns are daunting, no refunds for time,
Yet here we are, laughing at the climb.

Undefined Aspects of Authenticity

Rated stars and user reviews,
Searching for depth in byte-sized news.
But life's NFT can't be uploaded,
In a digital maze, our spirit's corroded.

Feelings on Prime? That's a fake sale,
Amazon can't ship what makes us prevail.
Brand new emotions, packed in a box,
But can you really trust those E-walking socks?

The Cart of Contemplation

Adding thoughts like it's retail therapy,
But do they come with a warranty?
Life's great questions, tossed like salad,
Spilling juice on wisdom lost in the ballad.

Checkout's a gamble, with no price tag,
Throwing in dreams, all tied in a rag.
Yet somehow we smile, what a delight,
For the journey itself is the funny bite.

Empty Boxes and Full Hearts

Clicking through life like a curious cat,
Unpacking the void—oh, imagine that!
An empty box, who knew it could hold,
A treasure of laughter, a sight uncontrolled?

Bubbles of joy from each popped mistake,
What's truly 'real' in the things that we make?
Maybe connection's the surprising deal,
Wrapped up in warmth, a comforting meal.

Flash Sales of the Heart

Click, click, what a steal,
Every deal feels surreal.
A heart on clearance, why so cheap?
Snagging joy while half-asleep.

Add to cart, but wait a sec,
What if love's a tiny speck?
Checkout line, a quirky fate,
Returns are free, but love? Don't wait.

Decrypting the Delay

Order placed, the clock ticks slow,
Was it a glitch, or just for show?
Where's that rush, the thrill of now?
Still in the cart, like a lost cow.

Tracking updates, it's a game,
My heart's on hold, but feels the same.
Did I forget to press 'pay'?
Or is this love's own delay?

The Wishlist for Wholeness

Add happiness, a sprinkle of glee,
But it's out of stock, just like me.
A cart full of dreams, oh what a sight,
But checkout's closed, so hold on tight.

Gift wrap laughter, a dash of fun,
But self-help books, I've too many, hon.
Why not just buy a sense of peace?
Sometimes the urge to shop won't cease.

Browsing the Unseen

I clicked through smiles, in pixels bright,
But reality lurks just out of sight.
What's the return policy for fate?
A laugh, a sigh, it's never too late.

In the clearance aisle, I search in vain,
Seeking meaning, oh what a pain.
Yet in humor, I find the key,
To laugh at life, now that's the spree!

Lost in Digital Aisles

Scrolling through the options galore,
Searching for joy, but I find a chore.
Clicking on gadgets I never will need,
Feeling so lost, in this digital creed.

Where's the aisle for fulfillment so bright?
All I see is a sale that feels just not right.
Add to cart dreams, but checkout feels grim,
Trying to shop for the meaning on whim.

The Price of Existence

I added my soul to the virtual cart,
But all I got was a pop-up for art.
Is it free shipping, or is there a fee?
Guess I'll just settle for memes, woe is me!

Life's not a product, can't use Prime for that,
Tried to fast-track joy, but it's all just a spat.
One-click laughter, two-click despair,
Checkout's a mess, who even cares?

Cart Full of Questions

My virtual cart's bursting with queries galore,
"What's the secret?" I shout, but they just ignore.
Adding "happiness" and "wisdom" with glee,
Yet my order's still pending, oh woe is me!

Wish there was a filter for meaning profound,
But all I find's a spatula, how is that sound?
I just need a clue or perhaps clear instruction,
Instead, I get socks—where's my reduction?

Virtual Dreams

I dream of rich moments, all wrapped up in pride,
But here's another ad that I really can't abide.
Swipe left on hopes for products I crave,
Life's no subscription, it's no digital rave.

Click here for joy, the algorithm sings,
Yet I'm left unfulfilled—such sad little things!
Chasing surreal deals just to feel a spark,
Instead, I find my heart numb and stark.

Real Disappointments

I ordered a guide to living it right,
But all that arrived was a toaster in sight.
"Not what I hoped," I sighed with a frown,
Why's it so hard just to wear a crown?

Is there an app for a laugh and a grin?
Or a download for joy—where do I begin?
The search for good times yields just empty space,
Return policy's clear: it's all just a race.

The Rent of Resolution

Searching for joy in a box,
I click and I scroll,
A click of a button,
But I'm left with a hole.

I add to my cart,
But the soul's still on sale,
No Prime shipping here,
Just a laugh and a wail.

I read all the reviews,
Five stars for a mug,
But I chug down my doubts,
In a drizzle of shrug.

In the end, I just find,
A quirk here and there,
A light-hearted spin,
But not what you wear.

Clicking Through Clarity

Searching for wisdom,
With a click of my mouse,
I find quirky gadgets,
And a cat-shaped house.

The algorithm knows,
What I'm wanting today,
A blender for smoothies,
Or a llama bouquet?

I filter by ratings,
But miss out on glee,
I can't seem to find,
What I need to be me.

As I add more items,
My wish list grows long,
But meaning is absent,
In this consumer song.

The Mysterious Menu of Meaning

Menu of purpose,
Filled with oddities,
I'm craving the truth,
But it's lost in the breeze.

I order a side,
Of laughter and peace,
But at checkout, alas,
All my choices decrease.

Maybe a platter,
Of memories bright?
But they're out of stock,
So I settle for light.

Dessert with some hope,
And a sprinkle of fun,
In this feast of existence,
Shall I just eat a bun?

Checkout Lines and Choices

Long lines of choices,
What a curious sight,
With a cart full of dreams,
And discounts on fright.

A coupon for wisdom,
If only it worked,
But the cashier just chuckles,
As my patience is perked.

Should I take the path,
Of the grown-up or child?
Each checkout a puzzle,
That leaves me beguiled.

I can count my regrets,
Like items on sale,
But in this comedy,
I still wish to prevail.

Shopping for Significance

Click, click, a cart is full,
Yet still, my heart's a dull pull.
I seek the great profound call,
But it seems I bought a rubber ball.

Filters set to 'life's grand quest',
Yet all I find is a cozy vest.
Where's the widget for the soul?
Just more socks – this can't be the goal!

With Prime I hoped to find delight,
Instead, I got a cat's new bite.
I added wisdom, love, and mirth,
But it shipped my hopes back to Earth!

In a sea of deals I feel so small,
Searching for more beyond the mall.
They say fulfillment's just a click,
But I think that's a dirty trick!

Pixels and Paradoxes

Scrolling through a pixelated haze,
Chasing meaning in a digital maze.
Each 'add to cart' feels like a joke,
Is enlightenment really a trendy cloak?

I browsed and browsed 'till my eyes went red,
Found a book titled 'Get Out of Your Head'.
But what if that wisdom's just a fun read?
And I'm left with a supplement for greed?

The paradox of choices galore,
Help or hoax? I can't take anymore!
I found a poster with sage advice,
But it's framed by my unfiltered vice.

In the reviews I see hope is sold,
But five stars can't buy back the old.
As I click, I giggle in despair,
Will my arrival arrive with flair?

E-commerce Epiphanies

I thought I'd find deep truths galore,
Just three clicks, I'd unlock the door.
But instead, I faced a shampoo set,
For vibrant hair? Oh, what a bet!

One-click chaos, like a fleeting thought,
I'll find my bliss in the latest pot.
Yet all I got was a gadget that sings,
No cosmic truth, just Wi-Fi strings.

In my search for the existential gem,
I stumbled on a board game for them.
Life lessons packed in every play,
But what if this game leads me astray?

As I surf through offers, my laughter rings,
An inflatable pool as joy's new wings!
Yet deep down, I know I still seek
More than vinyl and gadgets – that's my tweak.

The Unfindable Item

I clicked 'best-sellers,' 'top reviewed,'
Yet joy eludes and I feel subdued.
Is there a filter for dreams that stick?
All I see is a broom and a brick.

A thousand listings for epic adventure,
And yet, none of them feels like a mentor.
A spatula for flipping, but what's the use,
When I can't flip my own inner blues?

I searched for wisdom wrapped in foam,
But instead found a garden gnome.
Will my great purpose slip through the net?
An inflatable llama? Regret, I bet!

With checkout complete, I sit and stare,
At coupon codes for love and care.
But at the end of this click and chase,
Real meaning's lost in the shopping space.

Item Not Found in Reality

Clicking through the endless items,
But the heart keeps asking why.
A toaster's not a philosopher,
Yet here we are with baked rye.

Life's a cart that's never checked out,
With discounts on happiness, too.
I'm seeking peace in shipping boxes,
But all that's left is 'who knew?'

My thoughts are buried in the wishlist,
Searching for the joy on sale.
But refunding dreams is harder,
When a box of socks comes in male.

So here's to the items unlisted,
The joys that can't be ordered online.
For real meaning's found in laughter,
Not in an algorithm's design.

Reflections in the Refurbished Glass

I peered in a mirror and said,
'What's with the glare and smudges?'
No soap to cleanse this confusion,
Just a rant about all the drudges.

They say clarity comes at a cost,
But my last purchase was just a bag.
No shipment can show what I'm missing,
Except perhaps an old nag.

With every care package unopened,
I might find deep thoughts in there.
But instead, it's filled with old gadgets,
And a dust bunny race beyond compare.

So I toast to the clear reflections,
In glass that's chipped and not new.
Sometimes the heart finds itself dirty,
Laughs harder at the absurd view.

The Inventory of Introspection

In a warehouse stuffed with feelings,
I rummaged through the aisles of me.
So many boxes of memories,
Who knew I'd need a degree?

There's a shelf of dreams I never bought,
Next to shirts that don't quite fit.
A hat that says 'I know it all,'
And a dancing hula skirt bit.

I scanned for wisdom on clearance,
But all I found was old cheese.
I'm not sure if I'm alive yet,
Or just here for a series of jeez.

So let's price the laughter a little,
And put it right on display.
For clarity's always half-off,
In this goofy, chaotic ballet.

Rethinking Reality Beyond the Screen

Scrolling through the reels of life,
I bumped into a digital wall.
When did the pixels replace hugs?
And who ordered likes at the mall?

Widgets can't whisper secrets,
Nor can they sing to soothe souls.
Pressed 'play' on a life that feels scripted,
Where the heart's lost in pixelized holes.

I checked out the FAQ on emotions,
But the answers were all 404.
How can I download pure laughter?
When the punchlines are hidden in lore.

So I shut down my browser of worries,
And closed all the tabs of the mind.
Here's to the joys of reality,
The messy, the odd, the undefined!

Life's Unavailable Items

Searching for wisdom in a cart so wide,
But wisdom's one item that's long since defied.
I clicked on my dreams, all out of stock,
Just a message from fate: your hopes are a block.

I ordered a purpose, it shipped back to me,
With a label that read, 'Not meant to be!'
I browse through the options, a curious plight,
Yet the answers I seek aren't in black and white.

In the aisle of life, I'm lost in the views,
With returns on my heart, and no chance to choose.
Maybe next time I'll try a physical store,
But first, let me check my latest online score.

Clicking through laughter, and joy by the mile,
Yet the checkout for meaning just revokes my smile.
I'll keep navigating, with a wink and a grin,
For even the lost can still get a win.

Shipping Realizations

Placed my order for joy with a side of cheer,
But it's stuck in transit, oh dear, oh dear!
Out for delivery, my hopes drape on racks,
While patience runs low, and caution just cracks.

Tracking my spirit, it's lost in the void,
I refresh every hour, oh, how I'm annoyed!
The carrier's motto: 'Lost is not found,'
Guess my life's purpose is still underground!

I thought it was Prime, all quick and so slick,
But reality's shipping is often a trick.
The funny part's knowing, with each failed pursuit,
That wisdom in transit might still wear a boot.

So I jest with my fate, and I laugh in the rain,
For humor might just be the best way to gain.
Next time I'll order with less speed and fear,
And maybe my package will soon appear!

The Error 404 of Existence

Typed in my queries to find what I seek,
But the page came back with a message so bleak:
'Error 404: Deep thoughts not found,'
Just echoes of questions, silent and round.

I tried to connect through the web of my mind,
But the links are all broken, the search is unkind.
Advice from the sages is offline today,
While I'm stuck with a browser that leads me astray.

I hit refresh daily, with hope in the mix,
But the universe giggles, and plays its own tricks.
The wisdom I crave isn't in cyberspace,
It's tangled in laughter and joy's embrace.

So I'll close all the tabs and leave it to chance,
For sometimes the answers come not with a glance.
Let the bandwidth of life take me where it will,
In laughter, I'll find what's missing—until!

Virtual Items, Real Questions

Scrolling through life like a shopping spree,
With items I can't touch but wish I could see.
A cart full of dreams, but they never quite load,
Just pixelated hopes on a long, winding road.

I search for the answers, they show up as ads,
But all the suggestions just seem to go bad.
'Buy one, get one!' they lure with delight,
Yet the offer of truth stays out of my sight.

A wishlist of wisdom, I dream it's in stock,
But evading my grasp like a clever old fox.
With clickbait of meaning, I wade through the mess,
Caught in the shuffle of digital stress.

So I'll unwrap the laughter and gift myself grace,
Embrace all the questions I see in this space.
For while the real answers may never arrive,
The fun's in the searching, it keeps me alive.

Enigmas Wrapped in Plastic

In boxes piled up high, oh what a sight,
A blender for smoothies, but I can't blend right.
A book on meditation, but it's still in shrink,
I search for my purpose, can I pause to think?

A puzzle of pieces, with none that fit,
Like socks that go missing, a true shopping hit.
I bought a new mug, it's the size of my dreams,
Yet coffee spills over, or so it seems.

Emptiness in Abundance

With carts overflowing, I scroll and I laugh,
For wisdom can't come with a prime membership path.
A thousand unique items, an endless parade,
But where is the joy? I can't find it made!

Got gadgets and gizmos under my bed,
But no insight of value swirling in my head.
A shelf full of trendy, yet wisdom denied,
Just clutter and chaos from the frugal side.

Searching Beyond the Cart

I ponder, I click, as I scroll through the night,
For satisfaction's elusive, oh what a plight.
A yoga class coupon, a quirky new tee,
But deep down inside, I'm just searching for me.

Deals of a lifetime that beckon and call,
Yet here I sit, laughing, I've got nothing at all.
The perfect life's recipe, I thought I must bake,
But it's sold out of stock, oh for goodness' sake!

Echoes of an Empty Wishlist

My wishlist is bulging, with items galore,
Yet somehow I'm lost, like on a deserted shore.
I add all these treasures, still feeling low,
Could a dancing cactus solve my existential woe?

With checkout so tempting, the doorbell's a thrill,
But the joy is quite fleeting, like a caffeine chill.
A cart full of laughter, yet hearts need more cheer,
Maybe I'll just order a lifetime of beer!

Cybernetic Queries and Human Hearts

In a world of clicks and swipes,
Where meaning hides behind the types,
I search for wisdom's shiny face,
Yet find just socks in cyberspace.

The bots can't laugh, they can't cry,
They type and sell, but they don't try,
To know the heart, to feel the beat,
Instead they just recommend a seat.

A quest for joy in plastic bags,
With terms of service and all the tags,
But can't I trade my woes for laughs?
Or find a soul in all the drafts?

So here I scroll, I make my plea,
For joy, for life, not just a key,
To unlock treasures, deep and sweet,
A meaning only humans meet.

Carting Home What Can't Be Bought

In cardboard boxes, dreams reside,
Yet in the end, what's left beside?
A gadget here, a trend that fades,
But wisdom's lost in flashy shades.

I'm loading up on what seems fine,
Yet none of it is truly mine,
As prices soar and discounts fall,
Can joy be bought? I doubt it all.

I tried to add zest to my cart,
With special offers for the heart,
But found that love won't ship and sell,
It hides away in a well-worn shell.

So off I trot from virtual spree,
To laugh with friends and dance with glee,
For things that matter can't be rung,
Or read in lists, or ever sung.

Browsing the Soul

I scroll through life, past every deal,
Finding not what's truly real,
A match for socks, or pots for stew,
But searching for what's deep and true.

With every click, my heart does sigh,
As wishlist grows; but oh, the why?
A search for joy, in items grand,
Yet missing the touch of a kind hand.

The pages flash, they sure do gleam,
Yet none fulfill that ancient dream,
To sit and chat, to share a laugh,
Not just an order or an autograph.

So on I scroll, a hapless fool,
Neglecting life's most sacred rule,
That laughter's found in shared delight,
Not in the glow of a screen's bright light.

Beyond Reviews and Ratings

I read the stars, both five and one,
Yet still feel lost, I'm not the only one,
For wisdom won't come in a box,
Or in the words of random flocks.

A toaster's great, they all insist,
But where's the guide to love's twist?
The pins and needles of human art,
Can't be reviewed or sold apart.

I ponder deeply, check again,
The specials for my inner zen,
But searching stores won't lead the way,
To find a friend or start a play.

So let's put down the mouse and type,
And join a crowd, perhaps a hype,
For life's best moves defy the charts,
And flourish best in open hearts.

Checkout Dreams: An Empty Cart

In a digital maze, I roam each day,
Clicking and scrolling, I've lost my way.
Cart full of wishes, but missing the spark,
Just pixels and prices, where's the real heart?

I search for a meaning, a grand shiny prize,
But all I encounter are gadgets and lies.
A toaster that dances, a blender that sings,
Yet none of them answer the deep, thoughtful things.

Beyond Two-Day Delivery

Expecting deep wisdom in a cardboard box,
I tear through the tape, but it's just a pair of socks.
Two-day delivery doesn't fix my plight,
And no one's shipping joy overnight.

The guy at the door just shrugs with a grin,
He's seen me order all that junk again.
With each little package, my hopes crash and fall,
As the universe chuckles, 'It's just stuff after all.'

Searching for Purpose in Packaged Boxes

A prime number of items come to my door,
I rip at the wrapping, but just find the chore.
Each box holds the promise of joy, what a tease,
Yet inside them, I find only plastic and keys.

I bought a "Guide to Happiness," it came with a pen,
But the ink ran out fast, not a clue to depend.
Turns out the answers can't fit in a crate,
Who knew my quest for meaning would all have to wait?

The Illusion of Convenience

Oh, the wonders of shopping with just a few clicks,
Yet I still overload on the quarrels and tricks.
Convenience is king in this bizarre jungle,
But why do I feel like I'm in a fun jungle?

A life hack for happiness surely exists,
Just not in a package with ribbons and lists.
So I'll close my laptop, step outside with a cheer,
And find that the meaning isn't sold here, my dear.

Decode the Digital Delusion

Clicking through the shiny screen,
A treasure trove of things unseen.
But wisdom's not in Prime's next day,
It hides where laughter leads the way.

Searching gadgets, shiny and bright,
Will not reveal your guiding light.
The secret lies beyond the cart,
In moments shared, not goods to start.

With each delivery pause and sip,
The soul's true art is in the trip.
Not all that glitters comes with glee,
Find joy in chats, not just a spree.

So close the tabs, take a step back,
In all those pixels lies a lack.
Decode the web, but leave behind,
The superficial stuff that blinds your mind.

The Fragility of Online Fulfillment

I ordered joy, it came in a box,
But when I opened, it was just socks.
An echo of giggles, a phantom of cheer,
Yet still, I find no snicker here.

The reviews raved, five stars galore,
But clicking 'add to cart' is such a bore.
How fragile is the joy that's sold,
Like bubble wrap, it pops when cold.

Tracking shipped dreams down a digital lane,
Will never replace the warmth of rain.
Life's essence can't be boxed away,
In smiles and hugs, we find our play.

So let your heart roam far and wide,
Unwrap the laughter, the love, the ride.
Don't hinge your hope on clicks and rates,
For true fulfillment is what creates.

Unlisted Wonders and Forgotten Dreams

In a sea of products, bright and loud,
I seek for joy in every crowd.
But none come labeled, none come priced,
Unlisted treasures go unrecognized.

My dreams are stuck on a wish list plight,
While shipments of hope are lost in flight.
In clicks and swipes, I start to lose,
The beauty found in life's vast views.

Free returns? Well, thoughts don't ship,
As I type and type, my fingers slip.
But dreams don't need a two-day fate,
They flourish slow, they resonate.

So seek the wonders not in a browse,
But in the smiles beneath the brows.
Find hidden gems where laughter's schemes,
Outshine the pixels of borrowed dreams.

Exploring Existential Returns

Every search bar can't find the spark,
That lights the path through the dark.
The truth's not nested in algorithms tight,
But in the joy of a silly night.

In endless scrolling through life's sale,
I need a map, not a tracking trail.
Returns are easy for unused toys,
But laughter? That's one of life's true joys.

From checkout carts to fleeting buys,
I ponder a world beyond lost ties.
Our trips to the store can miss the beat,
When life's grand adventure is out on the street.

So step outside from the glowing chat,
Embrace the chaos, wear a silly hat.
Existence has refunds, but laughter remains,
In hearts' endless treasures, true joy sustains.

Missing Items on the Shelf of Life

Sometimes I browse the aisles with glee,
Searching for purpose, like a product spree.
But all I find are socks that don't match,
And books with titles promising a catch.

My cart is full of dreams on hold,
Yet no discounts on wisdom, truth, or gold.
I add some joy, a sprinkle of cheer,
But click 'checkout' and it disappears!

In the return section, I find dismay,
As laughter fades and hopes stray away.
A little chaos, a side of fate,
At the checkout line, I contemplate.

So I leave the store with a silly grin,
Knowing life's not found in a catalog win.
It's hidden in moments, not wrapped in string,
And the best things aren't listed—what joy they bring.

Transactions of Truth

In the digital age, I sought some sense,
With one-click orders, so quick, intense.
But truth isn't measured in stars or sales,
It's more like a story that often fails.

I filled my cart with ideas anew,
But at checkout, I found an error too.
The shipping took longer than I had planned,
As life's finest lessons slipped through my hand.

With a search for meaning that goes on and on,
I realize the answers are often a con.
There's no prime option for wisdom's delight,
It comes with a '404' to spark insight.

So I refresh my page with a sigh of relief,
And wander the web, seeking some belief.
In the great marketplace, it's laughter I trust,
For the best things in life come without a fuss.

Wishlist Woes and Wonders

I made a wishlist for joy and wit,
Thinking I'd find them, just a little bit.
I added some giggles, a sprinkle of cheer,
But the stock was low, alas, oh dear!

The laughter I sought wasn't available now,
I pondered my choices, furrowed my brow.
"Out of stock" on peace, "discontinued" on fun,
A ghost of fulfillment, lurking, it's done.

I clicked on the box for "add to cart,"
But deep down I knew, it's a bumpy start.
In the clearance aisle, I spotted a grin,
It whispered through chaos, "Let the fun begin!"

So I left the wishlist, my heart feeling light,
Finding joy in the now, embracing the night.
No need for a coupon or a deal so grand,
For the wonders of life are all in hand.

Shipping the Soul's Questions

I sent my inquiries across the net,
Hoping for answers, no need to fret.
But each reply came with more perplexed looks,
Like browsing for wisdom in outdated books.

"Next day delivery" was my eager promise,
But life held its packages, wrapped in suspense.
Confusing confirmations, no tracking number,
As I pondered the purpose, awake from my slumber.

I tried to exchange the woes in my heart,
But you can't find truth just by clicking 'start.'
The soul's greatest answers aren't bound by a list,
They float through the chaos, persist and twist.

So I'll wait for the mailman to come for a while,
With hopes on the horizon and a cheeky smile.
For the journey is funny, a grand ol' jest,
And life's little secrets are the very best.

Algorithms and Inner Journeys

Searching through lists, I scroll and scroll,
While deep in my heart, I lose all control.
Recommendations based on where I have been,
But wisdom and joy, they just can't be seen.

A cart full of gadgets, oh what a thrill,
Yet none of them cure my existential chill.
From smart fridges to drones, what luck I've amassed,
But true enlightenment? I seem to ask fast.

Every click brings a smile, a dopamine hit,
Yet answers to questions still seem so far split.
The wonder of searching, a digital maze,
But clarity's lost in a subscription craze.

So here I sit, lost in artificial bliss,
Where finding myself is a hit or miss.
Perhaps the best deals are just not for me,
For real life's adventures are free, you see!

Consumables of the Conscious Mind

With every new trend, I ponder and muse,
As I fill up my cart with special red shoes.
In search of enlightenment, oh what a quest,
Yet all I discover is a nap and a rest.

A subscription box full of snacks to delight,
Still leaving me hungry for deeper insight.
Chasing influencers, tips, and a plaque,
But wisdom, my friend, is never on track.

I binge on self-help, I click 'add to cart',
Yet wisdom and laughs just don't play their part.
Looking for meaning in spices and teas,
But finding fulfillment feels like a tease.

In this endless shopping, I giggle and grin,
For the things that we cherish must truly begin.
With a heart full of laughter, just pause for a while,
The best things are free, just follow your smile!

Wishlist of the Wandering Heart

A wish list of wonders to take me away,
To lands filled with joy and a sun-soaked display.
Yet every new gadget, it comes with a fee,
The price of contentment? A mystery to me.

I dream of a castle with walls made of gold,
But for now, it's just socks that I happen to fold.
Gadgets for travel, a compass, a map,
While my heart takes a journey; I slip into a nap.

The joys that I crave don't ship with my Prime,
Their value is found in savoring time.
As I put down my phone and gaze at the stars,
I realize that moments don't come in jars.

So here's to the wanderers, lost in the night,
Let's laugh at our lists in the soft, silver light.
For what we adore isn't sourced or deferred,
It blooms in the laughter and love that we've heard!

Hidden Treasures in the Human Experience

Scrolling for joy in a digital spree,
Searching for treasure in all that I see.
Each click is a promise of ease and of grace,
Yet life's truest gems are found face to face.

Who needs a subscription when laughter can bloom?
With friends by my side, we'll banish the gloom.
So I toss out my cart and I step out the door,
For connection's the gold that I'm truly here for.

With memes for our moments and snacks for our cheer,
There's richness in friendship that banishes fear.
So here's to the joy in the chaos and mess,
Where the hidden treasure is sweet happiness.

From sunsets to silliness, the hunt's never done,
Life's finest adventures come free and with fun.
So I'll leave all the packages, just come take a seat,
And let's find the meaning in shared laughs, oh so sweet!

Navigating the Aisles of Existence

In a store filled with gadgets and dreams,
I search for the spark, or so it seems.
But all I find are endless returns,
And the puzzles of life, still twisted in turns.

Amid the bright lights, I wander around,
A cart full of questions, no answers found.
Checkout lines stretch like eternal queues,
And where's the aisle for these existential blues?

The Price Tag of Purpose

I found a neat label stuck to a jar,
It promised me meaning—called it a star.
But when I clicked 'buy', it just sat on the shelf,
Guess purpose can't be replaced by a self-help book itself.

A sale on enlightenment is hard to resist,
But all that I got was a plot twist!
With discounts on wisdom, I gave it a shot,
But clarity's cost? You can't pay with a lot!

Digital Dreams and Distant Stars

I swiped through my options, a galaxy wide,
Searching for answers in a cosmic ride.
But all I found were memes and dogs,
Who needs deep thoughts when you can watch fog?

Click for new visions, just one more trend,
I bought into hopes that were bound to bend.
The cosmos is vast, yet my screen feels tight,
Lost in the pixels, forgot about flight.

Unpacking the Void

I ordered a package, believed it was gold,
Inside was a riddle, all wrapped up and cold.
Unpacking the void, it felt like a chore,
Wrapped in ambiguity, it wanted to explore.

Bubble wrap popped with truths we ignore,
Yet here in my hands—nothing but lore.
I checked for instructions, a guide on my fate,
But these came with no manual, just questions to sate.

Browsing for Belonging

In a sea of gadgets, I'm lost,
Searching for wisdom, what a cost.
Clicking through socks and gizmos galore,
Where's the manual for life I adore?

Cart full of dreams, but still I sigh,
A toaster can't teach you how to fly.
Checkout's a circus, a bright, buzzing hive,
But deep down I know, I'm just here to survive.

The Marketplace of Meaning

Scrolling through choices, my brain starts to ache,
Advice from a blender? That's a big mistake!
Maybe a mug could fill up my void,
But sipping from plastic leaves me paranoid.

In baskets of wisdom, it's all just a game,
With coupons for joy, but none quite the same.
Life lessons on sale, next day delivery,
But none are refundable, no matter the fee.

Unwritten Codes of Connectivity

Searching for answers, my screen starts to glow,
But emojis can't tell me what I need to know.
A digital party, with avatars to cheer,
Yet no one can listen or offer a beer.

Friends in the cloud, but alone in my room,
With likes and with shares, I still feel the gloom.
I try to connect, but the signal is weak,
Maybe I'll find depth in a TikTok sneak peek.

Floating Among Filtered Choices

Drowning in filters, it's hard to stay sane,
While influencers promise to ease all my pain.
Clicking on wellness, my mind starts to whirl,
They said it brings peace, but it's all just a swirl.

Finding a purpose, is it two-day prime?
Or a quirky subscription, wrapped up in a rhyme?
I add all the items, feeling more lost,
With every new feature, I'm counting the cost.

Packaging Purpose in a Digital World

In boxes wrapped, with ribbons bright,
We seek the truth in the online light.
Yet no prime shipping for the mind's quest,
Just giggles and clicks—what a strange jest!

Unbox your dreams with a cursor's stroke,
Yet wisdom eludes like an old tired joke.
Click and scroll through life's endless aisle,
With every search, just a pixelated smile.

Swiping left on the metaphysical grind,
Searching for meaning, but what will we find?
The heart's deep questions don't come in a box,
Just lighthearted chuckles and quirky old clocks.

So let's order pizza, ignore the plight,
And laugh at our wanderings under the digital light.
For purpose might not come tied up nice,
But laughter is surely a fair trade for price.

Anomalies in the Algorithm

In the realm of code, where logic should dance,
We chase our whims like a curious romance.
But algorithms giggle at our search for gold,
Suggesting pet rocks when our dreams unfold.

What's trending now? Rubber ducks and such,
But deep wisdom? Oh, not so much!
We scroll through selfies, and puppies in hats,
Wondering if life is just trading for chats.

With every click, we find something new,
But answers often come with a baffling view.
Instead of insights, we get meme-filled woes,
The algorithm mocks as the true path goes.

Yet still, we laugh at the quirks of this site,
As mystery lingers in the pixels of light.
For while searching for meaning, we might just find,
The joy of a laugh and the plunge of the mind.

Cart Contents of the Soul

In a digital cart, we load our desires,
Filling with hopes, like a kid in a choir.
A discount on happiness? What a sweet deal!
But checkout won't bring the heart's true appeal.

Click for fulfillment, toss in your dreams,
But the checkout page holds some silly schemes.
The universe laughs as we press 'add to cart',
Thinking new gadgets can fill up our heart.

Subscriptions for wisdom delivered each week,
Yet all we get is spam and a cheeky sneak peek.
Throw in some laughter, and an old comfy sweater,
Hoping it all might make us feel better.

So load up your cart with a quirky grin,
As life's little treasures are tucked deep within.
For joy isn't bought but rather it grows,
In the shared silly moments and love that we know.

Search Filters for the Heart

Filters applied on this search for the soul,
Adjusting the bright till we feel a whole.
But what's the rating on joy and delight?
Five stars on laughter, now that feels right!

Refine your needs to what truly matters,
But results keep popping like strange ancient patters.
Search for connection, but find another ad,
You'll laugh at the nonsense; oh, isn't it sad?

Options to choose, like flavors of cake,
But still, the connection is just a fake shake.
All we wanted was an empathetic hug,
Instead, we end up with a gag-worthy mug.

So let's browse through laughter and friendship galore,
For the heart's best filters create joy to explore.
And in this vast shopping spree of the soul,
The best finds in life are what make us whole.

www.ingramcontent.com/pod-product-compliance
Lightning Source LLC
Chambersburg PA
CBHW071827160426
43209CB00003B/224